ITALIAN COOKING... what passion!!!

ATS Italia Editrice

SUMMARY

MAIN COURSES

DESSERTS

PRESENTATION

Annibale Carracci, Il mangiatore di fagioli

Italian cooking... what passion!!! is the title that best conveys the joy with which one savors good Italian cuisine. The recipes in this book are simple, fast and photographed without tricks to help the reader cook without problems; to understand a culture one must live it, and to appreciate the cuisine one must cook it.

Cuisine is culture *when one produces it*, because man strives to create his own food and aspires to superimpose that which he produces over that which he gathers; it is culture *when one prepares it*, because man transforms the ingredients thanks to elaborative techniques and to fire; it is culture *when one consumes it*, because man, although omnivore, does not eat anything, he *selects* his own food according to criteria tied to many factors and values, some of which assume symbolic worth.

With this book, we wanted to let you all participate in that Italian Life Style in which Italian cuisine is an integral part and of which the whole world is envious!

Before I leave you to the recipes, I would like to recommend a few things: olive oil, pasta, rice, bread and cheese together with aromatic herbs and wine are the backbone of our cuisine.

Olive oil, to be trustworthy, must indicate the farmer and the production date; it must be consumed within 18 to 24 months; it is the opposite of wine: the younger it is the better.

Pasta is not a Chinese invention: the Greeks and later the Romans ate it over 3000 years ago. When Marco Polo returned from China, it was already produced both in Liguria as well as in Campania and the Arabs had already invented dry pasta.

One cooks pasta in abundant water (only water, no oil): 2.8 ounces of pasta, which is the correct portion, and 0.35 ounces of salt for every 2.75 cups of water. Salt is to be added once the water boils and pasta is to be added when the water resumes boiling. Stir the pasta immediately after.

For the cooking time, follow the manufacturer's instructions; stir and taste the pasta often. When it is cooked, remove the pasta from the fire and drain it, leaving it a little humid in order to pour it in a preheated container. Pasta is the Lady of the Table, she deserves the maximum respect and one must not make her wait!

Rice is not a side dish in Italian cuisine, it is the leading player and Risotto is the king of kings. To cook a good Risotto requires Carnaroli or Vialone Nano rice.

Italian cuisine is that of "Pane e Companatico," or rather of "bread and what you eat with it;" thinking about Italian cuisine without bread is like thinking about a beautiful woman without eyes! It is fundamental that bread is made with unrefined wheat flour.

Italy is rich with over 700 cheeses from cow, sheep, goat and buffalo milk. Many cheeses are the only type in the world like Parmesan, Mozzarella and Gorgonzola. Cheeses should be savored at room temperature, with some good bread and some good wine.

Italian cuisine changes according to the herbs, wines, oils and bread used in the diverse regions of Italy which are more than 20. Herbs enrich dishes with precious perfumes and flavors, but it is not good to use too many herbs in the same recipe because they are not easy to digest.

Wine is the opposite of oil, the older it is the better it is, but white wines are better in the first four years and reds in the first six. Italy is rich with precious wines from the Alps to Sicily. The ancient Romans said that a meal without wine is a "Prandium Caninum" a meal for the dogs, personally I agree with the ancient Romans and I hope that our readers agree with me!

Paolo Villoresi
President of the Italian Culinary Institute

STARTERS

fresh tomato bruschetta

(bruschetta romana)

ingredients
SERVES 4

- 4 ripe tomatoes, seeded and diced
- 2 tablespoons red onion, diced
- 2 tablespoons extra-virgin olive oil, plus extra
- ½ garlic clove
- 4 leaves fresh basil, torn into small pieces
- salt and freshly ground pepper
- 4 slices crusty Italian bread

preparation

In a small bowl, mix tomatoes with minced onion, 2 tablespoons of olive oil and the basil, and season with salt and pepper. • Lightly toast the bread on a grill or under the broiler, and rub with the cut side of the garlic. • Arrange the garlic toast on a platter, sprinkle with salt and drizzle generously with olive oil. • Spoonthe tomato mixture on top of each piece of toast, and serve immediately.

Rome, *Coliseum*

tuscan crostini

(crostini toscani)

ingredients
SERVES 4

- ¼ cup extra-virgin olive oil
- ½ large onion, chopped
- ¾ pound fresh chicken
- ¼ cup Vin Santo
  (or substitute dessert wine)
- 2 anchovy fillets packed in salt, rinsed
- 1 tablespoon capers packed in salt,
  rinsed and finely chopped, plus extra
- ¼ cup chicken broth, plus extra, heated
- freshly ground pepper
- 1 loaf Tuscan bread,
  cut into ¼-inch slices

preparation

Preheat the broiler. • In a large skillet over medium heat, warm the olive oil. • Add the onion, and sauté until translucent, about 5 minutes. • Add the chicken livers, and cook for about 10 minutes, stirring frequently to prevent sticking. • Deglaze with the Vin Santo, and cook until it evaporates. • Transfer the liver mixture to a food processor, and process until smooth. • Return the liver mixture to the skillet, and add the anchovies, capers and ¼ cup of the warm chicken broth. • Season with pepper, and cook for about 15 minutes, adding more broth if the mixture is dry. • Return to the food processor, and process until smooth. • Set aside. • Toast one side of each bread slice under the broiler until golden. • Spread the chicken liver mixture on the toasted side. • Pour some hot broth into a shallow dish, and briefly dip the un-toasted side of each slice in the broth. • Top the crostini with some whole capers, and serve immediately.

Florence, *Santa María del Fiore*

stuffed rice balls

(supplì)

preparation

ingredients
MAKES 16

- 1¾ cup boiled rice cooked al dente (or leftover risotto)

FOR THE RAGÙ AND FILLING

- 1 tablespoon extra-virgin olive oil
- 1 small onion, diced
- 1 carrot, peeled and diced
- 1 stalk celery, diced
- ½ pound ground lamb
- ½ cup red wine
- 1 cup canned whole, peeled tomatoes, drained and chopped
- 4 ounces fresh mozzarella, cut into 16 small cubes
- 3 eggs, beaten
- salt and freshly ground pepper
- 1 cup bread crumbs
- olive oil for frying

FOR THE RAGÙ

In a skillet, heat extra-virgin olive oil. • Add onion, celery, carrot and lamb; stir until meat is cooked through and onion is translucent. • Deglaze with wine. • Add tomatoes; cook until ragù reaches a dense texture. • Add salt to taste. • Season the boiled rice with ragù and let it cool down.

FOR THE RICE BALLS

With wet hands, form 16 balls of seasoned rice or leftover risotto. • Poke a hole in each ball with your thumb, and make a little space inside. • Fill each one with a chunk of mozzarella. • Seal the opening with another dollop of seasoned rice or leftover risotto. • Roll each ball in beaten egg, then bread crumbs seasoned with salt and pepper. • Warm olive oil over medium-high heat in a heavy-bottomed pot. • Deep-fry in batches until golden-brown. • Drain on paper towels. • Serve immediately.

Rome, *Trinità dei Monti*

mozzarella in carrozza

preparation

Place the flour in a bowl, and season it with salt and pepper. • Lay ½ of the slices of the bread on a flat work surface. • Top each with a slice of mozzarella and ½ anchovie. • Top with a piece of bread, and dip each sandwich in the milk. • Dredge each sandwich in the seasoned flour, shaking off the excess. • In a large skillet with high sides, warm 1 inch of olive oil until shimmering. • In a bowl, beat the eggs, and season with salt and pepper. • Dip each sandwich into the beaten egg mixture. • Carefully place each sandwich into the skillet with the hot oil, and fry until golden on each side. • Remove from skillet, drain on paper towels and sprinkle with additional salt before serving.

ingredients
SERVES 4

- flour for dredging
- salt and freshly ground pepper
- 8 slices white bread, crusts removed, cut in ½ diagonally
- 4 thick slices fresh mozzarella, cut in ½ diagonally
- 2 anchovy fillets, chopped
- ½ cup cold whole milk
- olive oil for frying
- 2 eggs

The Vatican City, Saint Peter's Basilica

panzanella

preparation

ingredients
SERVES 6

- 1 2-day-old country loaf or baguette, thickly sliced and torn into 1-inch pieces
- 6 ripe plum or vine-ripened tomatoes, seeded and chopped
- 1 red onion, chopped
- 2 cucumbers, seeded and chopped
- ½ small bunch basil, chopped
- salt and freshly ground pepper
- ¾ cup extra-virgin olive oil
- ¼ cup red wine vinegar

Put the stale bread pieces in a bowl with 1 cup of cold water. • Soak until the bread absorbs water and softens. • Working with a little of the bread at a time, remove any excess water by squeezing the pieces gently in your hand. • Place the softened bread in a large salad bowl and add the rest of the chopped vegetables and basil. Season with salt and pepper. • In a small mixing bowl, add the vinegar and slowly whisk in the olive oil until combined. • Drizzle salad with dressing to taste and toss well. • Chill the salad in the refrigerator until ready to serve. • Before bringing the salad to the table, add some more dressing and garnish with basil.

Florence, *Ponte Vecchio*

fagioli all'uccelletto

preparation

ingredients
SERVES 4

- ¼ cup extra-virgin olive oil
- 1 28-ounce can peeled tomatoes, drained and roughly chopped
- 1 pound dried cannellini beans
- 2 cloves garlic, finely chopped
- 2 fresh sage leaves
- salt
- freshly ground pepper

Soak the dried cannellini beans in cold water overnight and drain them. • Put the cannellini beans into a pot and cook until tender. • Let them cool into their own cooking liquid. • In a large skillet with high sides, warm the olive oil over medium-high heat. • Add garlic and sage, garlic to become golden allow and sauté for 4 minutes. • Drain the beans and add them to the skillet, season with salt and pepper and cook for a couple of minutes. • Add the tomatoes and cook for 30 minutes over low heat, stirring every now and then with a wooden spoon. • The beans will be tender but firm.

Florence, *View*

amalfi seafood salad

(insalata di mare Amalfi)

ingredients
SERVES 8

- 1 pound octopus, cleaned
- 1 pound squid, cleaned
- 1 pound lobster
- 1 pound bay scallops
- 1 pound medium shrimp, cooked and deveined
- 1 pound lump crab meat
- ¼ cup extra-virgin olive oil, plus extra
- 1 clove garlic, minced
- 2 tablespoons parsley, chopped, divided
- juice of 2 lemons, divided
- salt and freshly ground pepper

preparation

Put a large pot of water over high heat, and when it boils, add salt. • Add the squid, and cook for 10 minutes. • Check to make sure it's tender, remove with a slotted spoon and set aside. • Add the octopus, and let cook for 5 minutes. • Check to make sure it's tender, remove with a slotted spoon and set aside. • Add the squid and cook for 1½ to 2 minutes. • Check to make sure it's tender, remove with a slotted spoon, and set aside. • If any of these fish are still rubbery after their allotted cooking time, continue to cook until tender (50 to 60 minutes). • Boil lobsters for about 8 minutes. • Remove from water, and plunge into a bowl filled with ice water. • Steam scallops over simmering water until just cooked through, about 8 to 10 minutes. • Plunge cooked scallops into ice bath. • Allow each to cool, and then cut into bite-sized pieces. • Remove lobster meat from shell, cut into small chunks and toss all the fish (including the cooked crab and shrimp) in a large mixing bowl, and add the olive oil, garlic, 1 tablespoon parsley and the juice of 1 lemon. • Season with salt to taste. • Mix thoroughly, and refrigerate overnight. • Before serving, add more olive oil, the remaining lemon juice and parsley.

The Amalfi coast, *View*

STARTERS

summer seafood salad

(insalata di mare estiva)

preparation

Bring a large pot of water to a boil.
• Add the calamari, and cook for 15 seconds. • Remove the calamari from the water, and plunge into a bowl of ice water. • Drain, and set aside. • Add the shrimp to the boiling water, and cook for 3 minutes. • Drain, and set aside to cool. • Place the mussels in a pot, and add ¼ cup of water. • Place over medium heat, cover, and cook for about 4 minutes or until the shells open. • Discard any mussels that don't open. • Drain, and set aside to cool.
• In a bowl, combine the calamari, shrimp, mussels, celery and parsley.
• In a separate small bowl, whisk together the lemon juice and olive oil until emulsified. • Season with salt and pepper, add to the seafood, and mix well.

ingredients
SERVES 4

- 1 pound frozen or fresh calamari (defrosted if frozen), cleaned and thinly sliced
- 2 pounds medium shrimp, peeled and deveined
- 1 pound mussels, scrubbed and debearded
- 1 stalk celery, thinly sliced
- 2 tablespoons chopped parsley
- juice of 1 lemon
- 3 tablespoons extra-virgin olive oil
- salt and freshly ground pepper

Naples, *Castel dell'Ovo*

spaghetti al pomodoro

ingredients
SERVES 4

- 2 pounds ripe tomatoes
  (or 1 28-ounce can peeled
  Italian tomatoes)
- 5 tablespoons extra-virgin olive oil
- 1 clove garlic
- 1 small onion, diced
- 10 leaves fresh basil,
  chopped or torn into pieces
- salt and freshly ground pepper
- parmesan cheese
- 1 pound spaghetti

preparation

Bring a large pot of water to a boil. • Make a shallow "X" with a knife at the stem end of each tomato. • This will help you peel them later. • Drop the tomatoes into the boiling water, and cook for about 15 to 30 seconds. • Drain, and set aside until cool enough to handle. • Remove the tomato skin (it should peel right off). • Cut the tomatoes in half and scoop out the seeds. • Chop the remaining tomato flesh and reserve in a bowl (if using canned tomatoes, just pour into a bowl and use a fork or knife to cut them into smaller pieces). • In a large skillet, warm the olive oil over medium heat. • Add the whole garlic clove, and allow to become golden. • Remove the garlic clove, and add the diced onion. • Sauté until the onion becomes tender and translucent. • Add the tomatoes. • Season with salt and pepper, and turn heat down to low. • Cover, and allow to simmer for at least 30 minutes or up to one hour. • When ready to use, toss in the fresh basil. • Meanwhile, bring a large pot of water to a boil. • Add salt and the pasta and cook until al dente. • Drain the pasta, then add it to the sauce and toss well to combine. • Sprinkle the spaghetti with some parmesan cheese and serve.

Naples, *Fountain of the Immacolatella*

penne all'arrabbiata

ingredients
SERVES 4

- 2 tablespoons extra-virgin olive oil
- 2 cloves garlic, crushed
- ½ teaspoon crushed red pepper flakes
- 18 ounces peeled tomatoes, seeds removed
- salt
- 1 tablespoon chopped parsley
- 14 ounces penne pasta

preparation

Bring a large pot of water to a boil. • In a large skillet over medium-high heat, warm the oil. • Add the pepper flakes and the garlic cloves, and sauté until they soften and turn golden. • Remove and discard the garlic and pepper flakes, and add the tomatoes. • Season with salt and cook for 15 minutes. • While the sauce is cooking, salt the water and add the pasta. • Cook the pasta until al dente, drain, and transfer the pasta to the skillet with the sauce and toss it over medium-high heat. • Transfer the pasta into a heated serving dish and sprinkle it with the chopped parsley.

Rome, *The Capitol*

bucatini alla amatriciana

ingredients
SERVES 4

- 5 ounces guanciale (available at gourmet stores) or bacon, chopped
- 3 ripe tomatoes, peeled, seeded and chopped
- ½ teaspoon crushed red pepper flakes
- salt and freshly ground pepper
- 14 ounces bucatini pasta
- ⅓ cup pecorino romano, grated
- extra-virgin olive oil

preparation

Bring a large pot of water to a boil.
• In a saucepan over medium-high heat, add the extra-virgin olive oil and the guanciale and cook until the meat slightly crisps, 6 to 8 minutes.
• Remove the guanciale and set aside.
• Add the tomatoes to the pan, then add the crushed red pepper flakes and season with salt and pepper. • Cook for 10 minutes, then return the guanciale pieces to the sauce to reheat. • While the sauce is cooking, salt the water and add the pasta. • Cook the bucatini until al dente, drain and toss with the sauce.
• Top with the pecorino and serve warm.

Rome, *The Roman Forum*

spaghetti with tomatoes, capers, and mozzarella
(spaghetti alla Bellini)

ingredients
SERVES 4

- 5 ripe tomatoes, washed and chopped
- 1 tablespoon capers packed in salt, rinsed
- salt and freshly ground pepper
- 1 pound spaghetti
- 8 ounces fresh mozzarella (or substitute regular mozzarella), cubed
- 2 tablespoons chopped basil
- 3 tablespoons extra-virgin olive oil

Taormina, *Greek Roman Theatre*

preparation

Combine the tomatoes and capers in a bowl. • Season with salt and pepper, and set aside. • Drain the tomato mixture, reserving the liquid. • In a separate bowl combine the mozzarella with the basil, and season with salt and pepper. • In a skillet over medium heat, warm the olive oil, and add the tomato mixture. • Bring a large pot of water to a boil. • Add salt and the pasta, and cook until al dente. • Drain the pasta, and add it to the sauce. • If the sauce is too dry, add some of the reserved liquid from the tomatoes. • Toss and remove from the heat. • Add the mozzarella mixture, toss, and serve.

taglierini with peas and truffle

(taglierini ai piselli e tartufo)

preparation

- 2 cans petite peas
- 2 tablespoons extra-virgin olive oil
- 1 clove garlic, sliced
- 1 scallion, minced finely
- 1 tablespoon parsley, minced
- 1 cube chicken bouillon
- ½ teaspoon white pepper
- 1 tablespoon butter
- 1 pound taglierini egg pasta
- salt
- white truffle

Open and drain the peas, rinse them gently with lukewarm water and let them drain again. • In a pan, heat the olive oil with the garlic, scallion, parsley, peas, bouillon cube and pepper, stirring constantly. • After 3 minutes, add ¼ cup of water and bring to a boil. • Lower the flame and simmer for 5 minutes. • Add the butter and allow to melt. • Meanwhile, bring a pot of water to a boil and add the pasta and salt. • Cook until the pasta is al dente and drain well. • Add to the saucepan, allow the pasta to absorb the sauce, and serve with a few thin slices of white truffle on the top.

Urbino, *View*

FIRST COURSES

linguine with clams

ingredients
SERVES 4

- 1½ pounds littleneck clams, soaked in cold water for 30 minutes, drained
- salt
- 1 pound linguine
- 2 tablespoons extra-virgin olive oil
- 1 clove garlic, peeled
- ½ cup white wine
- freshly ground pepper
- 1 tablespoon chopped parsley

preparation

Place the clams in a pot with 1 cup of water. • Cover, and place over medium heat for 4 minutes, or until they open. • Drain, reserving the cooking liquid. • Bring a large pot of water to a boil. • Add salt and the pasta, and cook until al dente. • In a skillet over medium heat, warm the olive oil. • Add the garlic, and sauté for 1 minute. • Discard the garlic clove, and add the wine and reserved cooking liquid. • Season with salt and pepper, and simmer until reduced slightly. • Drain the pasta, and add it to the skillet along with the clams. • Garnish with the parsley, and serve.

Rome, *Coliseum and Arch of Constantine*

tagliolini with shrimp and squid in garlic sauce

(tagliolini calamari e gamberetti)

ingredients
SERVES 4

- 8 ounces squid
- 3 tablespoons extra-virgin olive oil
- 8 ounces shrimp, peeled and deveined
- 1 clove garlic
- salt and freshly ground pepper
- ⅛ teaspoon hot red pepper flakes
- ½ cup dry white wine
- 1 pound tagliolini, or substitute linguine
- 2 tablespoons parsley, chopped, plus extra for garnish

preparation

Separate the squid bodies from the tentacles and set the tentacles aside. • Remove and discard the cartilage and ink sack from the bodies. • Slice the bodies into rings and set them aside. • In a large skillet over medium-high heat, warm the olive oil. • Add the squid rings and tentacles, the shrimp and garlic and sauté for about 8 minutes. • Season with salt, pepper and the hot red pepper flakes and stir. • Deglaze with the white wine and cook, stirring, until the wine starts to evaporate, about 4 minutes. • Cover and reduce the heat to low.
• Meanwhile, bring a large pot of water to a boil.
• Add salt and the pasta and cook until al dente.
• Drain and transfer the pasta to the skillet with the squid and shrimp mixture. • Sprinkle with the chopped parsley, toss and serve.

Naples, *Maschio Angioino*

orecchiette with broccoli rabe

ingredients
SERVES 4

- 2 pounds broccoli rabe, trimmed
- salt
- 1 pound orecchiette pasta
- 2 tablespoons extra-virgin olive oil, plus extra
- 1 clove garlic, peeled
- crushed red pepper flakes
- 2 anchovy fillets, packed in salt, rinsed and finely chopped

preparation

Bring a large pot of water to a boil. • Wash the broccoli rabe, and drain. • Salt the water, and add the broccoli rabe and the pasta. • Cook until the pasta is al dente. • Meanwhile, warm the olive oil in a large skillet over medium heat. • Add the garlic clove, and sauté until it softens and turns golden, about 2 to 3 minutes. • Add a pinch of the red pepper flakes and anchovies. • Drain the pasta and broccoli rabe, and add them to the skillet. • Cook another minute, toss, and serve. • Drizzle the top with olive oil.

Alberobello, *Church of St. Anthony*

sardinian gnocchetti with sausage ragù

preparation

ingredients
SERVES 6

FOR THE PASTA

- 1 pinch saffron
- 4 cups semolina flour
- salt
- all-purpose flour for dusting

FOR THE RAGÙ

- 3 tablespoons extra-virgin olive oil
- 1 small onion, chopped
- 1 clove garlic, minced
- 2 sweet Italian sausages,
  casings removed, crumbled
- salt and freshly ground pepper
- 3 leaves basil, chopped
- 1 16-ounce can crushed tomatoes
- ½ cup freshly grated pecorino
  (or substitute domestic romano)

La Maddalena, *view*

FOR THE PASTA
Soak the saffron in ¾ cup warm water for 10 minutes. • On a large work surface, mound the semolina flour, and make a well in the center. • Add the saffron water and a pinch of salt, and mix well with a fork. • Add more warm water a little bit at a time, and knead until the dough is smooth, about 5 minutes.• Pull off a piece of dough the size of a golf ball, keeping the rest covered. • On a work surface dusted with all-purpose flour, roll the dough into a ¼-inch-thick rope. • Pull off small pieces of dough, and curl each piece over your finger. • Sprinkle the pasta lightly with flour, and let it dry.
FOR THE RAGÙ
In a skillet over medium heat, warm the olive oil. • Add the onion, garlic and sausage. • Sauté for 5 minutes, season with salt and pepper, and add the basil and tomatoes. • Simmer for 10 minutes.

• Boil the pasta in salted water, about 6 to 8 minutes. • Drain, toss with the ragù, and sprinkle with grated cheese.

tagliatelle al ragù

preparation

ingredients
SERVES 4

- 3 tablespoons extra-virgin olive oil
- 1 small onion, diced
- 1 carrot, peeled and diced
- 1 stalk celery, diced
- 1 pound lean ground beef chuck
- salt and freshly ground pepper
- ½ cup red wine
- 1 28-ounce can whole tomatoes
- 3 tablespoons chopped parsley
- 4 cups beef stock
- 1 pound tagliatelle
- 1 cup freshly grated grana padano

In a saucepan over medium-high heat, warm the olive oil. • Add the onion, carrot and celery, and cook until tender, about 5 minutes. • Add the beef, season with salt and pepper, and cook for 10 minutes, stirring to scrape up any brown bits from the bottom of the pan. • Deglaze with the wine, and cook until it begins to evaporate. • Add the tomatoes, crushing them while stirring. Add the parsley, and cook for another 10 minutes. • Add the beef stock, adjust seasonings, and lower the heat. • Simmer until the sauce is rich and thick, for 45 minutes to 3 hours.• Bring a pot of water to a boil. • Add salt and the pasta and cook until al dente. • Drain the pasta, add it to the sauce, and toss. • Serve topping every plate with the grated grana.

Bologna, *Piazza Maggiore*

lasagna with beef ragù

preparation

FOR THE LASAGNA

- salt
- 1 pound lasagna noodles
- 1 tablespoon extra-virgin olive oil, plus extra
- 4 cups basic meat sauce
- 2 cups freshly grated grana padano (or substitute domestic parmesan)
- parsley for garnish

FOR THE MEAT SAUCE

- 3 tablespoons extra-virgin olive oil
- 1 small onion, diced
- 1 carrot, peeled and diced
- 1 stalk celery, diced
- 1 pound lean ground beef chuck
- salt and freshly ground pepper
- ½ cup red wine
- 1 28-ounce can whole tomatoes
- 3 tablespoons chopped parsley
- 4 cups beef stock

FOR THE MEAT SAUCE

In a saucepan over medium-high heat, warm the olive oil. • Add the onion, carrot and celery, and cook until tender, about 5 minutes. • Add the beef, season with salt and pepper, and cook for 10 minutes, stirring to scrape up any brown bits from the bottom of the pan. • Deglaze with the wine, and cook until it begins to evaporate. • Add the tomatoes, crushing them while stirring. • Add the parsley, and cook for another 10 minutes. • Add the beef stock, adjust seasonings, and lower the heat. • Simmer until the sauce is rich and thick, for 45 minutes to 3 hours.

FOR THE LASAGNA

Preheat the oven to 350°. • Bring a large pot of water to a boil. • Add salt and the lasagna noodles, and cook until al dente. Drain, drizzle with olive oil, and set aside to cool. • Assemble the lasagna: spread out a layer of lasagna noodles in the bottom of an oiled 8-inch square baking dish. • Cover with a layer of meat sauce, and sprinkle with the grana. • Repeat the layering, until all the meat sauce has been used. • Finish with a layer of noodles, and a generous sprinkling of grana. • Place in the oven, and bake for 45 minutes. • Remove from the oven, and allow to rest for 10 minutes. • Slice, and serve garnished with parsley.

Bologna, *Sanctuary of St. Luca*

saffron risotto

ingredients
SERVES 4/6

- 3 tablespoons butter, divided
- 1 onion, diced
- 1 ½ tablespoons ox marrow
- salt and freshly ground pepper
- 2 cups Arborio rice
- 2 teaspoons saffron threads
- 8 cups boiling chicken stock, divided
- ½ cup freshly grated parmigiano reggiano (or substitute domestic parmesan)

preparation

In a pot over medium heat, melt 2 tablespoons of butter and 1 ½ tablespoons of ox marrow. • Add the onion and sauté until soft, about 6 minutes. • Add the rice, and sauté, stirring to coat thoroughly with butter, about 3 minutes. • Add 1 cup of stock to the rice and season with salt. • Continue adding stock in 1-cup increments, stirring until the liquid is absorbed before adding more. • When the rice is al dente, add the saffron melted in two scoopfuls of stock and finish to cook the rice. • Remove the pot from the heat, and stir in the remaining butter, the parmigiano and some freshly ground pepper.

Milan, *Dome*

acquacotta

(Tuscan egg soup)

ingredients
SERVES 4

- ¼ cup extra-virgin olive oil
- 1 medium onion, diced
- 1 chili pepper, minced
- 1 stalk celery, cut into ¾-inch pieces
- 6 plum tomatoes, diced
- 4 slices crusty Italian bread
- ¾ cup freshly grated pecorino toscano (or substitute domestic parmesan)
- 4 eggs

preparation

In a heavy-bottomed pot over medium-low heat, warm the olive oil. • Add the onion, chili pepper, celery and tomatoes, and cook for 30 minutes. • Add 4 cups of warm water, and bring to a boil for 5 minutes. • Gently break the eggs into the pot being careful not to break the egg yolks. • Lightly toast the bread slices, and place them in the bottom of 4 bowls. • Sprinkle with the pecorino, and break one egg into each bowl. • Ladle the acquacotta into each bowl, and serve immediately.

Florence, Palazzo Vecchio

potato gnocchi with porcini mushroom sauce

FIRST COURSES

preparation

ingredients
SERVES 6

FOR THE SAUCE

- 1 cup dried porcini mushrooms
- ¼ cup extra-virgin olive oil
- 2 small shallots, minced
- ½ cup dry white wine
- 1 cup heavy cream
- salt and freshly ground pepper
- sage for garnish

FOR THE GNOCCHI

- 2½ pounds potatoes
- 1 tablespoon salt
- 1½ cups flour, plus extra
- ⅛ teaspoon nutmeg
- 1 egg (optional)

Milan, *Dome Square*

FOR THE SAUCE

In a bowl, combine the porcini with 1 cup of boiling water and set aside to soak for 30 minutes, or until softened. • Remove the mushrooms, squeeze out any excess water and chop them. • Strain the remaining water through a cheese cloth. Reserve the water and set aside. • In a large skillet over medium-high heat, warm the olive oil. • Add the shallots and mushrooms and sauté for about 4 minutes. • Deglaze with the wine. • Cook until the wine reduces by ½, about 18 minutes. • Add the cream and reserved mushroom liquid. • Let the liquids reduce again by ¼, about 5 minutes. • Season with salt and freshly ground pepper.

FOR THE GNOCCHI

In a large pot over high heat, combine the potatoes with enough cold water to cover and bring to a boil. • Add salt and cook the potatoes, skin on, for about 20 minutes, or until tender when pierced with a knife. • While the potatoes are still hot, peel and press them through a ricer onto a clean flat work surface dusted with flour. Allow to cool.• Sprinkle with 1½ cups flour. • Using your hand and a dough scraper, combine potatoes and flour until a dough begins to form. • Add the nutmeg and continue to knead. • Add the egg only if the dough fails to come together. • Knead until the dough is soft and smooth.• Cut the dough into thirds, and using ⅓ at a time, roll dough into long, even ropes. • Cover the unused dough with plastic wrap while you work so it doesn't dry out. • Cut the dough ropes into 1-inch pieces, and roll each piece off the grooves of a gnocchi board or the tines of a fork to create a grooved texture.

• Meanwhile, bring a pot of water to a boil, add salt and the gnocchi. • Cook the gnocchi until they float to the surface and remove with a slotted spoon. • Add the gnocchi to the pan with the sauce and toss well to coat. • Garnish with sage to serve.

pasta e fagioli

preparation

- 3 15-ounce cans cannellini beans, rinsed and drained
- 3 tablespoons extra-virgin olive oil,
- 1 clove garlic, minced
- 4 sage leaves
- ⅔ cup diced tomatoes
- salt and freshly ground pepper
- ½ pound jumbo pasta shells

Purée 2 cans of cannellini beans until smooth. • In a deep skillet over medium heat, warm 3 tablespoons of olive oil, add the garlic and sauté until golden. • Pour in the bean mixture and add 6 cups of water. • Season with salt and pepper. • Add the diced tomatoes and, when the cooking is almost done, mix in the can of whole cannellini beans. • Bring to a boil. • Add the pasta and cook until al dente. • Serve the soup hot, lukewarm or cold.

Bologna, *Garisenda and Asinelli towers*

pasta e ceci

ingredients
SERVES 4

- 8 ounces dried chickpeas, soaked in water overnight and drained
- 1 sprig of rosemary or (as an alternative) 2 bay leaves
- 1 pound lagane or pappardelle pasta
- 3 tablespoons extra-virgin olive oil
- 1 clove garlic
- 2 ounces sun-dried or peeled tomatoes, roughly chopped
- salt and freshly ground pepper

preparation

Place the chickpeas in a pot. Cover with water, and add salt. • Simmer over medium-low heat for about 3 hours. • When half cooking time is passed, remove 2 spoonfuls of chickpeas and purée until smooth. • Return the chickpeas mixture into the pot and continue to cook for the remaining time. • In a deep skillet over medium heat, warm 3 tablespoons of olive oil, add the rosemary, the garlic and the chopped tomatoes and cook for 10 minutes. • Turn off the heat, remove the garlic and pour this sauce into the pot with the chickpeas, stir and add salt, if necessary. • Add the pasta and cook until al dente.
• Place the soup in a serving bowl and season with olive oil and pepper.

The Vatican City, *Saint Peter's Basilica*

veal in tuna sauce
(vitello tonnato)

preparation

ingredients
SERVES 4/6

FOR THE VEAL
- 1 piece veal bottom round, about 2 pounds
- 3 tablespoons extra-virgin olive oil
- 1 carrot, chopped
- 1 stalk celery, chopped
- 1 potato, cubed
- salt
- 2 cups beef broth, heated

FOR THE SAUCE
- 1 egg
- 1 cup extra-virgin olive oil
- juice of 1 small lemon
- 1 6-ounce can tuna, drained
- 3 tablespoons capers
- 2 anchovies, chopped

FOR THE VEAL
Preheat the oven to 350°. • In a heavy-bottomed, oven safe pot over high heat, warm the olive oil. • Add the veal and cook until golden on all sides. • Add the carrots, celery, potatoes and season with salt. • Transfer the pot to the oven to cook for 30 minutes, or until cooked through. • Check the roast periodically to make sure it doesn't get too dry. • If dry, add the broth ½ cup at a time. • Remove the veal from the oven, discard the butcher's string and slice thinly.

FOR THE SAUCE
In a food processor combine the egg, extra-virgin olive oil and lemon juice. • Add the tuna, capers and anchovies and purée until smooth. • To serve, slice the veal and place the slices on a serving platter. • Pour the tuna sauce over the veal and garnish with some capers.

Turin, *Mole Antonelliana*

ossibuchi alla milanese

preparation

ingredients
SERVES 4

- 4 veal marrow-bones
- flour
- ½ cup butter
- 1 tablespoon extra-virgin olive oil
- 1 cup dry white wine
- ½ onion, minced
- 1 inch tomato concentrate
- 2 cups water and 1 cube bouillon
- salt and freshly ground pepper
- ½ bunch parsley, chopped
- 2 anchovy fillets packed
  in salt, rinsed
- 1 clove garlic
- zest of 1 lemon

Cut the film that covers the marrow-bones in 2/3 points in order to prevent them from curling while cooking and dredge each marrow-bone in flour. • Add the butter, the extra-virgin olive oil and the onion to a large skillet. • Cook over medium-low heat until soft. • Remove the onion and sauté the veal marrow-bones until browned. • Add the white wine, season with salt, pepper and the tomato concentrate melted in half cup of warm water and readd the onion.• Simmer over medium-low heat for 1½ hour, stirring it often to prevent from sticking to the bottom of the skillet. • Add some stock if necessary. • In the mean time prepare the famous "gremolada", by chopping together the parsley, 1 clove of garlic, the anchovy fillets and the lemon zest. • Add the "gremolada" to the skillet when the remaining cooking time is only 5 minutes. • Add 1 last scoopful of stock, turn over the ossibuchi and here you are... the ossibuchi alla milanese are finally ready. • Serve hot accompanied by saffron risotto (see p. 44).

Milan, *La Scala Theatre*

saltimbocca alla romana

ingredients
SERVES 8

- 3 ounces prosciutto, thinly sliced
- 8 sage leaves
- 8 slices of veal, 6 to 8 ounces each
- ¼ cup flour
- 4 tablespoons butter
- ¾ cup dry white wine
- salt and freshly ground pepper

preparation

Place half a slice of prosciutto on each slice of veal and top with a sage leaf. • Cover with plastic wrap. • On a clean work surface, pound the veal slices with a meat mallet to ¼-inch thick, until the prosciutto and sage are embedded in the veal. • Dust both sides with flour. • In a large skillet over medium-high heat, warm the butter and arrange the veal slices in the pan. • Sauté the veal until golden brown on both sides. • Remove the veal from the skillet and place in a serving platter. • Add the wine to the skillet and scrape up any browned bits from the bottom of the pan. • Simmer over medium-high heat until it thickens slightly. • Pour the sauce over the saltimbocca, and serve.

Rome, *Capitoline She-Wolf*

arista

ingredients
SERVES 8

- 1 pork loin, about 3 pounds, bone in
- 2 cloves garlic
- 3 tablespoons fresh rosemary, leaves only
- 2 tablespoons fresh sage
- salt and freshly ground black pepper
- 3 tablespoons butter
- ½ cup extra-virgin olive oil
- ¼ cup white wine
- 2 pounds baby potatoes cut in slices

preparation

Preheat the oven to 400°. • Mince the garlic, rosemary, and sage and mix with the salt and the pepper. • Divide this mixture in two equal parts and mix one half with the butter using a fork. • Mix the other half with 3 tablespoons of the oil. • Lift the pork up vertically on one end, and with a sharp and narrow knife, cut a long hole through the middle of the pork. • Make sure you do not cut all the way through to the other end. Enlarge the cut with a wooden spoon. • Stuff the opening with the butter and herb mixture, pushing it all the way in with wooden spoon. • Fill the entire cavity in this manner. • Using butchers string (that you have soaked in warm water beforehand), tie the loin rather tightly, starting from the end at which you made the cut. • Cover the outside of the meat and bone with the oil and herb mixture. • Place in a roasting pan loin along with the remaining olive oil. • Put the pan in the oven. • After 1 hour and 20 minutes, add the potatoes to the pan, stirring well to coat with olive oil and meat drippings. • After 15 minutes, add the wine to the pan, stirring to coat the potatoes. • Allow to cook for 10 more minutes. • Remove from the oven and serve hot.

Florence, *Basilica of Santa Maria Novella*

MAIN COURSES

abbacchio alla cacciatora

ingredients
SERVES 4/6

- 2 cloves garlic, crushed
- 1 teaspoon rosemary, chopped
- 2 anchovies, roughly chopped
- 1 cup white wine vinegar
- 2 pounds leg of spring lamb (suckling lamb), cut into ¾-inch pieces
- salt and freshly ground pepper
- ¼ cup extra-virgin olive oil
- 1 cup dry white wine

preparation

Using a mortar and pestle or a blender, crush garlic, rosemary and anchovies into a paste. • Add the vinegar a little at a time, stirring until the sauce is well blended. • Transfer to a bowl and cover. • In a skillet over medium-high heat, warm the olive oil and add the lamb pieces seasoned with salt and pepper. • Sauté until well browned on all sides. • Pour in the wine and bring to a simmer, then add the vinegar sauce. • Reduce the heat, cover and cook for 2 hours, stirring often. • Allow to sit for at least 30 minutes before serving.

Rome, *The Trevi fountain*

MAIN COURSES

florentine steak

ingredients
SERVES 4

- 1 Porterhouse steak, approximately 2¾ pounds, at least 1 inch thick
- salt and freshly ground pepper
- extra-virgin olive oil
- lemon juice

Florence, *Ponte Vecchio*

preparation

Make sure the steak is at room temperature. • Prepare a charcoal grill, and allow the coals to burn down until covered with a layer of gray ash. • The coals should be very hot, but you should see no flames. • Place the steak on the grill. • Allow to cook for 3 minutes, and turn over. • Sprinkle cooked side with salt, and allow to cook the other side for 3 minutes and then salt. • The amount of time a steak is cooked is a personal preference, but real Florentine steak must be rare cooked: the outside is gray-brown and the middle is red and slightly warm. • Season with freshly ground pepper, and serve with extra-virgin olive oil and lemon juice at the table.

MAIN COURSES

triglie al forno

(roasted red mullet)

preparation

Preheat the oven to 400°. • Season the fish on both sides with salt and pepper, and place skin-side down on a lightly oiled baking sheet. • Drizzle with the lemon juice, and sprinkle with the oregano.
• Bake in the oven for about 10 minutes.
• Serve over salad greens, and garnish with cherry tomatoes and lemon wedges.

ingredients
SERVES 4

- 8 red mullet fillets, skin on, about 4 ounces each
- salt and freshly ground pepper
- extra-virgin olive oil for
- greasing
- juice of 2 lemons, plus extra wedges for garnish
- 1 teaspoon dry oregano
- salad greens for garnish
- cherry tomatoes, halved, for garnish

Florence, *Basilica of Santa Croce*

pizza margherita

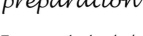

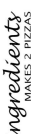

ingredients
MAKES 2 PIZZAS

- 8 cups all-purpose flour, plus extra
- 1 package active dry yeast
- 2 teaspoons salt
- 5/6 tomatoes, peeled and chopped
- 2 tablespoons extra-virgin olive oil, plus extra
- ½ teaspoon salt
- ¼ teaspoon pepper
- 2 tablespoons chopped basil
- 8 ounces fresh mozzarella, sliced
- extra-virgin olive oil

preparation

To prepare the dough place the flour and salt in a large bowl. • Proof the yeast in a separate bowl with 1 cup warm water. • Pour the yeast mixture into the bowl with the flour and salt, and mix. • Knead the dough, and add more flour or water if necessary until it reaches a soft consistency. • Place in an oiled bowl, cover, and let rise at room temperature until doubled in size, about 2 hour. • Punch the dough down, divide it in half, and form into two balls. • Cover with a clean dish towel, and let rise for 30 minutes. • Preheat oven to 350°. • Oil two 12-inch round pizza pans with high sides. • Stretch the dough onto the pans. • Spread some chopped tomatoes over each dough circle and oil generously. • Bake for 15 to 20 minutes. • Take out the pans, top with slices of mozzarella cheese and 2 tablespoons of chopped basil, season with salt, pepper and oil and bake until crisp, about 7 to 8 minutes. • Serve very hot.

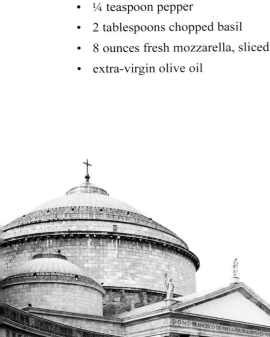

Naples, *Basilica of Saint Francis of Paola*

chocolate cream crostata

ingredients
SERVES 6 / 8

BASIC PASTA FROLLA
The quantities below yield a 12-inch crostata crust, or an 8-inch crust with lattice decorations.

- 1 egg
- 1 egg yolk
- 2¼ cups flour
- 1 stick unsalted butter, chilled and diced
- ⅓ cup plus 1 tablespoon sugar
- ⅛ teaspoon salt
- zest of 1 lemon, grated
  CHOCOLATE CREAM CROSTATA
- 1 recipe basic pasta frolla
- ¾ cup chocolate cream, plus extra

Ravenna, *Mosaic in the Mausoleum of Galla Placidia*

preparation

BASIC PASTA FROLLA
Hand method: In a large bowl, combine all the ingredients and work them with your hands. • When it starts to come together, transfer to a work surface and knead for a few seconds. • Transfer to a piece of plastic wrap. • Seal the dough inside the wrap and push it together so that there are no crumbs. • Flatten into a disk shape and transfer to the refrigerator to chill for 30 minutes, or until firm.
Food processor method: In a food processor, combine all of the ingredients and pulse until a ball begins to form. • Transfer onto a piece of plastic wrap and proceed as described above. • Line a tart pan with parchment paper. • Roll out the dough to ¼-inch thickness and carefully transfer to the pan. • Mold the bottom and sides of the dough so they fit in the pan, then prick the dough with a fork. • Remove any excess dough from the edges of the mold with a knife or your fingers.
CHOCOLATE CREAM CROSTATA
Prepare the crust according to the basic pasta frolla recipe. • Preheat the oven to 375°. Spread a thin even layer of chocolate cream over the pasta frolla line tart pan. • To make the lattice, roll out the remaining dough and cut into thin strips. • Lay the strips on top of the filling in even rows to make a grid. • Transfer to the oven to bake for 35 to 45 minutes. • Remove from the oven, then using a pastry bag, pipe chocolate cream rounds into the grids.

schiacciata con l'uva

ingredients
SERVES 6

- 1 tablespoon active dry yeast
- salt
- ¾ cup sugar
- ½ cup extra-virgin olive oil
- 3 cups unbleached all-purpose flour
- 2 pounds seedless black grapes

preparation

In a large bowl, dissolve the yeast in 1 cup of warm water. • When the mixture foams, stir in a pinch of salt, 4 tablespoons of sugar and 4 tablespoons of olive oil. • Stir in enough flour to make a soft dough that is not sticky. • On a lightly floured surface, knead the dough for 5 to 8 minutes, until firm smooth and elastic. • Place the dough in a bowl and cover it. • Set the dough aside to rise in a warm place for about 1 hour. • Preheat the oven to 375°. • Oil a rectangular baking sheet. • Transfer the dough to a lightly floured work surface and using a rolling pin, roll it out into a rectangle, about ⅛-inch thick. • Enough dough should hang over the edge of the pan to completely cover the top when folded. • Transfer the dough to a baking sheet. • Spread most of the grapes over it, drizzle with 2 tablespoons of olive oil and sprinkle with 2 tablespoons of sugar. • Fold the overhanging dough up over the grapes, covering them completely. • Press lightly to seal. Scatter the remaining grapes over the dough, drizzle with the remaining olive oil and sprinkle with the remaining sugar. • Bake until the dough is golden brown, about 45 minutes. • It's good to eat it hot or at room temperature, but the real recipe suggests to eat it the next day.

Florence, David by Michelangelo

castagnaccio

preparation

ingredients
SERVES 8

- 3 cups fresh chestnut flour
- 1 cup milk
- ¼ cup sugar
- salt
- 3 tablespoons extra-virgin olive oil, plus extra
- 2 tablespoons pine nuts
- 1 tablespoon fresh rosemary, leaves only

Preheat oven to 350°. • Sift the chestnut flour into a mixing bowl. • Add the milk and 2 cups of water, whisking constantly to avoid lumps. • The batter should be smooth and liquid. • Add the sugar, a pinch of salt and 3 tablespoons of extra-virgin olive oil, and mix well. • Oil a round or square cake pan, and pour in the batter (the batter should come less than 1 inch up the side of the pan). • Sprinkle with 2 tablespoons of pine nuts and 1 tablespoon of rosemary leaves, and drizzle with a little olive oil. • Bake for 40 minutes. • Serve at room temperature.

Florence, *View from Piazzale Michelangelo*

tiramisù

preparation

- 8 medium eggs, separated
- 1 cup sugar
- 1 pound mascarpone
- 1 cup brewed espresso
- ⅓ cup rum (optional)
- 25 ladyfinger cookies
- bitter cocoa powder for dusting

In a bowl, combine the egg yolks with the sugar. • Using a hand mixer, blend on high speed for 3 minutes. • Add the mascarpone, and beat for 2 minutes, or until the mixture is uniform and creamy. • Set aside. • In a clean bowl, beat the egg whites with a hand mixer until stiff peaks form. • Gradually fold the beaten egg whites into the mascarpone mixture. • Assemble the tiramisù: in a bowl, combine the espresso and the rum (optional). • One by one, dip the ladyfingers in the coffee mixture, and arrange them in a single layer along the bottom of an 8-inch square baking dish. • Spread a thin layer of mascarpone cream on top, followed by another layer of coffee-dipped ladyfingers. • Continue until you have 3 layers of ladyfingers, and finish with a layer of mascarpone cream. • Cover with plastic, and refrigerate overnight. • To serve, slice into squares, and sprinkle with cocoa powder.

Treviso, *Aerial view*

sicilian cannoli

preparation

ingredients
SERVES 4

- 1 pound fresh ricotta, drained
- ¾ cup confectioners' sugar, plus extra
- ¾ cup assorted candied fruit (lemons, oranges, cherries), chopped, divided
- ½ cup semisweet chocolate, finely chopped, plus extra
- 1 tablespoon orange-flower water
- 12 pre-packaged cannoli shells

In a bowl, combine the ricotta with the confectioners' sugar, ½ cup of the candied fruit, the chocolate and orange-flower water, and mix until the mixture is smooth. • Spoon the mixture into a pastry bag, and pipe into the cannoli shells. • Sprinkle the remaining ¼ cup of the candied fruit and some chopped chocolate over the filling at the edges of the cannoli. • Arrange the cannoli on a platter, and set aside in the refrigerator for 1 hour. • To serve, dust with confectioners' sugar.

Agrigento, *Concodia Temple*

© Copyright 2008 ATS Italia Editrice s.r.l.
All rights reserved

this volume has been edited and realized by
ATS Italia Editrice s.r.l.
via di Brava, 41/43 - 00163 Roma
tel. 0666415961 - fax 0666512461 - www.atsitalia.it

editing *Paola Ciogli*
iconographic researches *Angela Giommi*
graphic project, paging and book-cover *Roberta Belli*
scanning and chromatic corrections *Leandro Ricci*
technical coordinator *Flavio Zancla*

in cooperation with the *Italian Culinary Institute*:
person in charge *Paolo Villoresi*
consultant for the English version *Elisa Della Barba*

photographs:
Italian Culinary Institute, New York
PhotoService Electa, Milano
ATS Italia Editrice, Roma - (Mallio Falcioni)

Special thanks to Katia Rosa for her kind help

Questo volume è disponibile anche in lingua italiana
Ce volume est disponible aussi en français
Esta obra también está publicada en español
Dieser Band ist auch in deutscher Sprache erhältlich
Данное издание опубликовано также на русском языке

ISBN 978-88-7571-638-7

Printing:
Kina Italia/Lego - Italy